PROPHETIC
Heart Beat

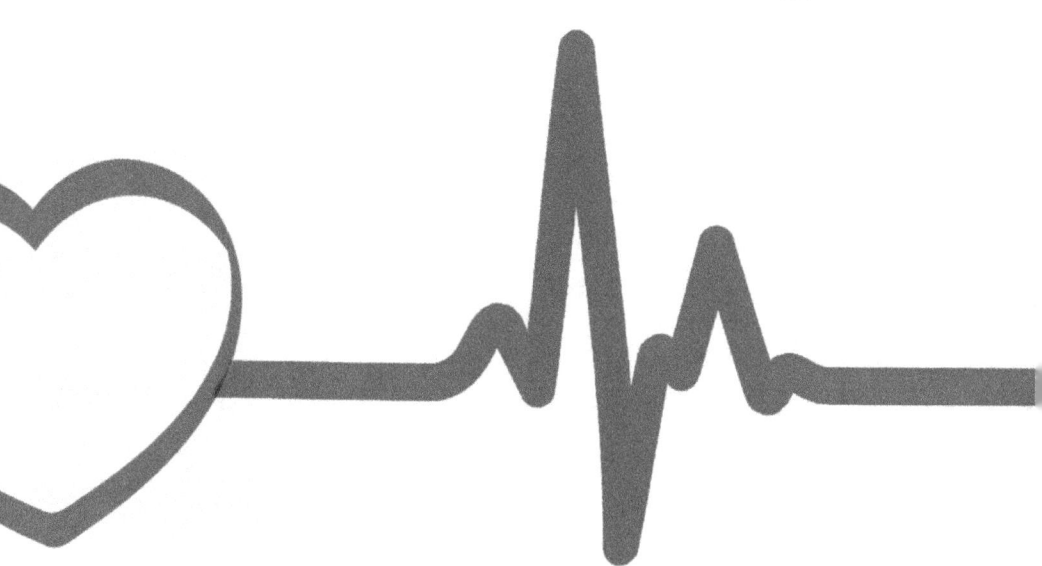

DR. JAMES E. RANDOLPH

Other Books by Dr. James E. Randolph

The Love Covenant

The Marriage Covenant Handbook

Destiny Dynasty Legacy

God Thoughts

Books Coming Soon by Dr. James E. Randolph

Endangered Species

The Word of Life

The ABC's of Salvation

Leadership 101

Unless otherwise noted all Scriptures taken from the New King James Version®. Copyright © 1982 by Thomas Nelson. Used by permission.

All rights reserved.

Scripture quotations taken from the Amplified® Bible (AMP), Copyright © 2015 by The Lockman Foundation Used by permission. www.Lockman.org.

Scripture quotations taken from the Amplified® Bible (AMPC),

Copyright © 1954, 1958, 1962, 1964, 1965, 1987 by The Lockman Foundation. Used by permission. www.Lockman.org.

Scripture quotations marked (NLT) are taken from the Holy Bible, New Living Translation, copyright ©1996, 2004, 2015 by Tyndale House Foundation. Used by permission of Tyndale House Publishers, Inc., Carol Stream, Illinois 60188. All rights reserved.

Graphics Licensed through Adobe Stock:
133506214

Gotham Books
30 N Gould St.
Ste. 20820, Sheridan, WY 82801
https://gothambooksinc.com/
Phone: 1 (307) 464-7800

© 2022 Dr. James E. Randolph. All rights reserved. No part of this book may be reproduced, stored in a retrieval system, or transmitted by any means without the written permission of the author.

Published by Gotham Books (September 22, 2022)

ISBN: 979-8-88775-065-1 P
ISBN: 979-8-88775-066-8 E

Any people depicted in stock imagery provided by iStock are models, and such images are being used for illustrative purposes only.

Certain stock imagery © iStock.

Because of the dynamic nature of the Internet, any web addresses, or links contained in this book may have changed since publication and may no longer be valid. The views expressed in this work are solely those of the author and do not necessarily reflect the views of the publisher, and the publisher hereby disclaims any responsibility for them.

Contents

Prophetic Heartbeats Day One
The Heart, Part One ------------------------------------ 1

Prophetic Heartbeats Day Two
The Heart, Part Two ------------------------------------ 5

Prophetic Heartbeats Day Three
What Is Prophecy? --------------------------------------- 9

Prophetic Heartbeats Day Four
Prophetic People --- 13

Prophetic Heartbeats Day Five
Prophetic Prayers Of The Heart. Part One ----------- 17

Prophetic Heartbeats Day Six
Prophetic Prayer Of The Heart, Part Two ----------- 21

Prophetic Heartbeats Day Seven
A Heart Of Trust, Part One ---------------------------- 25

Prophetic Heartbeats Day Eight
A Heart Of Trust, Part Two ---------------------------- 29

Prophetic Heartbeats Day Nine
Do Not Lose Heart, Part One -------------------------- 33

Prophetic Heartbeats Day Ten
Do Not Lose heart Part Two --------------------------- 37

Prophetic Heartbeats Day Eleven
We Rest, Part One -------------------------------------- 41

Prophetic Heartbeats Day Twelve
We Rest, Part Two -------------------------------------- 45

Prophetic Heartbeats Day Thirteen	
Healing From A Broken Heart, Part One	49
Prophetic Heartbeats Day Fourteen	
Healing From A Broken Heart, Part Two	53
Prophetic Heartbeats Day Fifteen	
The Peace That Guards Your Hearts, Part One	57
Prophetic Heartbeats Day Sixteen	
The Peace That Guards Your Hearts, Part Two	61
Prophetic Heartbeats Day Seventeen	
Don't Give Up Today	65
Prophetic Heartbeats Day Eighteen	
Walking With A Pure Heart	69
Prophetic Heartbeats Day Nineteen	
Do Doubt In My Heart, Part One	73
Prophetic Heartbeats Day Twenty	
No Doubt In My Heart, Part Two	77
Prophetic Heartbeats Day Twenty-One	
Hope Deferred	81
Prophetic Heartbeats Day Twenty-Two	
Desire	85
Prophetic Heartbeats Day Twenty-Three	
Failure Is Not Final, Part One	89
Prophetic Heartbeats Day Twenty-Four	
Failure Is Not Final, Part Two	93
Prophetic Heartbeats Day Twenty-Five	
Harden Not Your Heart, Part One	97
Prophetic Heartbeats Day Twenty-Six	
Harden Not Your Heart, Part Two	101

Prophetic Heartbeats Day Twenty-Seven
The Worshipper In You, Part One ---------------------- 105

Prophetic Heartbeats Day Twenty-Eight
The Worshipper In You, Part Two ---------------------- 109

Prophetic Heartbeats Day Twenty-Nine
A Heart Filled With The Voice Of God, Part One ------ 113

Prophetic Heartbeats Day Thirty
A Heart Filled With The Voice Of God, Part Two ------ 117

Prophetic Heartbeats Day Thirty-One
Prayer The Power Of An Excellent Spirit ---------------- 121

Conclusion --- 125

Your Finale Thoughts ------------------------------------ 126

PROPHETIC
Heart Beat

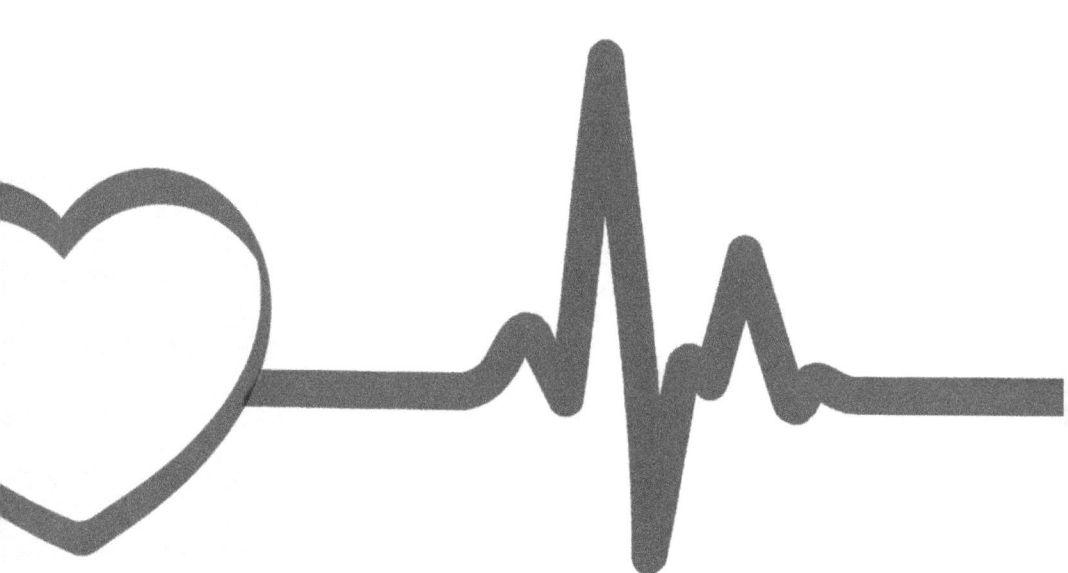

DR. JAMES E. RANDOLPH

Day One
The Heart, Part One
As a he thinks in his heart, so is he.
Proverbs 23:7a

Do you really know your heart? Do you understand how it will affect your entire life? Your heart is so vitally important to you and to God. You cannot take your heart for granted, ignore it or expect it to lead and guide you in the right direction on its own. God views your heart as the most important part of your entire life because it is His main area of focus and development in your life.

In 1 Samuel 16:7, the Lord is speaking to Samuel as he is faithfully trying to fulfill the assignment given to him from the Lord. His instructions are to go to the house of Jesse and anoint for Him the King that He chooses. Unfortunately, Samuel allows his natural eyes to get in the way. So, the Lord has to correct him and make known to him the way in which He looks at a man and chooses a King for Himself. Samuel is not only on assignment from God and for God, but he is also in training.

But the Lord said to Samuel, "Do not look at his appearance or at the height of his stature, because I have rejected him. For the Lord sees not as man sees; for man looks at the outward appearance, but the Lord looks at the heart."

I Samuel 16:7 AMP

In the Greek version of the Old Testament, the word heart here is the Greek word Cardiac. This word means: thoughts, reasoning, and understanding, will affections and emotions. We can see that the heart is not a part of your body, but rather it is an operating system. Your heart is your internal system that allows you to see, think feel and understand how to function through life. Jesus comes to enter into that system so that our operating system will whole heartedly repent and submit to the heart of God. Our system is to fully submit to God's Kingdom, operating system.

When this happens, the Lord will no longer see our old carnal heart, but rather He will see the heart of His Son, the Lord Jesus. As our heart surrenders to the heart of God, we will began to move in the prophetic life. This is the life God has prepared for us to live and enjoy. This is what Prophetic Heartbeats is all about. You and I are always in training and development before the Lord. So, don't get stuck on being right or in trying to be perfect, but keep your heart open and ready.

Prophetic words for your heart:

For I know the plans and thoughts that I have for you,' says the Lord, 'plans for peace and well-being and not for disaster, to give you a future and a hope.

Jeremiah 29:11 AMP

Meditation-Prayer-Reflection
DAY ONE

How did God speak to you today?

_____

_____

Day One

_____

_____

_____

_____

_____

_____

What are your thoughts now?

_____

_____

_____

_____

_____

_____

_____

How will you pray?

_____

_____

Day Two

The Heart, Part Two

As a he thinks in his heart, so is he.

Proverbs 23:7a

God is not biased. He is not judgmental toward His people, and He is not focused on the outside of man. This is something we should learn from Him which can make a huge difference in our lives. We are taught and trained to be outside minded and to judge based on what we see. As we get older these old roots and teachings get imbedded into our hearts and we become that person. Even Samuel, the great prophet of God, was guilty of this same type of biasness. He was biased when he thought that Jesse's first-born son fit the description of a king. But where did he get that description from? It was obvious that he did not get it from God; he had to have picked it up in the atmosphere in which he had grown up.

The environment that we grow up in contributes to the development of our hearts. That process makes us who we are. Yet the deeper question remains, "Is that really who we are in the context of God's plan and intent for us? Is our identity hidden from us because we have been shaped and molded by family teachings and habits? Are we victims of our environment that has taught us retaliation, fear, jealously, vanity and selfishness? Is pride really a part of the God identity that may not be working in your life?"

The scripture says, "As a he thinks in his heart, so is he". Consequently, the thoughts of your heart can make you somebody that you were never intended to be. So, stop and think about who you have become. What are your thoughts; do you like what you see? If you don't, then I am sure that God is not pleased. It's time to stop complaining, the whining and get over it. You can still become the person that God intended.

The process of changing when you have concluded you don't like the person you are now. The next point is to realize it's not for you to fix you. Yes, you are not the repair person, but you know the one who is. Start by bowing your head and surrender your heart and ask Him for a new heart. Stay open and get into the word of God allowing the Holy Spirit to read the word of God to you. Allow Him to speak to you and reveal great things.

Prophetic word for your heart:

"It is finished! All is complete, and the struggle is over. It will get easier for you!

Meditation-Prayer-Reflection
DAY TWO

How did God speak to you today?

_____

_____

_____

_____

_____

_____

___

___

___

What are your thoughts now?

___

___

___

___

___

___

___

___

How will you pray?

___

___

___

___

Day Three

What Is Prophecy?

Have you ever asked yourself, "What is prophecy? What if I told you that you were prophetic? What would you think? Would you think I was crazy? Would you think I had not heard from the Lord? Would it be more acceptable to say to you that you are not prophetic?

Prophetic Heartbeats is about God, you, and prophecy. Let's get an understanding of prophecy from a biblical standpoint. We all know that prophecy is the ability to foretell that which is to come. It is the ability to speak forth that which is not yet seen. It is the releasing of the unseen world into the seen world before it is visible. Prophecy is the prediction of that which is to come. To be a prophetic person may mean that you can predict the future. You also have the ability to be used of God to foretell and to reveal that which is to come. It means that God can reveal things to you and tell you to release them to others.

Another way to look at prophecy is it uncovers, reveals, unfolds, makes clear, makes known and brings forth that which is not seen or known. I would say that we are prophetic people. Why? Because we are the people of God who are being revealed, coming forth, living lives

that are being uncovered and made known. Our relationship with the Lord is constantly revealing the reality about ourselves. The uncovering and the foretelling of our lives is a daily manifestation of the work of the Spirit of God. The Holy Spirit is showing us each day the reality about ourselves. The revelation of our spiritual identity is being released daily as we draw near to God and depend on Him.

10 Romans 8:29-30 AMPC says; "For those whom He foreknew [of whom He was aware and loved beforehand], He also destined from the beginning [foreordaining them] to be molded into the image of His Son [and share inwardly His likeness], that He might become the firstborn among many brethren. And those whom He thus foreordained, He also called; and those whom He called, He also justified (acquitted, made righteous, putting them into right standing with Himself). And those whom He justified, He also glorified [raising them to a heavenly dignity and condition or state of being]."

Prophetic words for your heart:

"Today is the best day of your life, so declare it so! New life and new breath are in you today. I bring new refreshing and new confidence to you today! Believe it!"

Meditation-Prayer-Reflection
DAY THREE

How did God speak to you today?

_____

_____

_____

_____

_____

_____

_____

What are your thoughts now?

_____
_____
_____
_____
_____
_____
_____

How will you pray?

_____
_____
_____
_____

Day Four
Prophetic People

For whom He foreknew, He also predestined to be conformed to the image of His Son, that He might be the firstborn among many brethren. Moreover, whom He predestined, these He also called; whom He called, these He also justified; and whom He justified, these He also glorified.

Romans 8:29-30

a. God foreknew us

b. He destined us with divine predestination

c. We are destined to be molded in the image of Christ

d. We are brothers of Christ with Him being the first born

e. We are foreordained

f. We are called by God

g. We have been justified in Christ

h. We have been glorified in Christ

Each of these eight points outlined in Romans 8:29-30 clearly confirm that we are prophetic people. God foreordained, predestined, and purposed our creation and existence before there was any manifestation of our physical existence. We are yet being uncovered, revealed, and made known. Everyday God is showing us our true selves. It is not yet fully revealed who we really are, but there is the daily prophetic foretelling of our predestined future.

Our spiritual identity is yet a mystery to us. God is constantly moving and working in our lives to bring forth a manifestation of our true reality. We are made in the image and the likeness of God according to Genesis 2:26. The sacrificial and redemptive work of Christ is based upon the identity and purpose of a predestined, prophetic people. Everything about our prophetic identity in this world and the next comes from God. We are not our own, but we have been bought with a price.

Prophetic Heartbeats is written to bring you into awareness of how the Lord sees you and what the Lord has predestined for His prophetic people. You are not an accident, but you were born for a purpose and with purpose from the Lord.

Your prophetic destiny is unfolding. It is being revealed daily as you fully embrace and cooperate with the Holy Spirit as He supernaturally works the works of God within you. You are more than just a physical being; you are a living spirit; you have a soul, and you live in a body. Your life has eternity within your born-again spirit. The God life lives on the inside of you. So, relax, open your heart, and enjoy the journey as we explore Prophetic Heartbeats.

Prophetic words for your heart:

"Stop messing around with your fleshly nature; stop feeding the old man. You are fearfully and wonderfully made by your Creator and Designer. You are beautiful and a delight in His sight."

Meditation-Prayer-Reflection
DAY FOUR

How did God speak to you today?

_____

_____

_____

_____

_____

_____

_____

_____

What are your thoughts now?

_____

_____

_____

_____

_____

_____

_____

How will you pray?

_____

_____

_____

_____

Day Five

Prophetic Prayers of the Heart, Part One

Then the king said to Araunah, "No, but I will surely buy it from you for a price; nor will I offer burnt offerings to the Lord my God with that which costs me nothing.

2 Samuel 24:24a

We have been molded, developed, and shaped by our experiences in this world. Our minds have been trained and set on the course of logic, reason, and rationalization. Our life experiences have left us without spiritual revelation, passion, or pursuit towards God. Therefore, we find ourselves struggling to find God and ourselves in a deeper and more intimate way. We must come to realize that we have moved from a position of visitation to a place of habitation where divine revelation is released. We are new creatures created in Christ with a new DNA.

Prophetic prayer is praying out of our born-again spirit and not from our head. If you are struggling with prayer, it is because you are making prayer a head matter rather than a heart matter. Prayer is spiritual; it is to be born out of our spirit rather than out of our head. It is full of all kinds of desires, concerns, and ideas. Our head has an abundance of thoughts; it can be extreme and go off in another direction at anytime.

On the other hand, our born-again spirit is made in the image and the likeness of God. It already has within it the prophetic nature of God. Our Christ centered spirit stays in ready mode and remains in a spiritual posture with a prophetic appetite. The prophetic is not new, nor strange and not some sort of unknown requirement that your spirit resists. It has godly desires; it craves godly pleasure with its greatest yearning of wanting to please the Lord.

Prayer is not a burden, a chore, or a struggle for our spirit. It has a prophetic appetite to pray and to make contact with God. When our spirit cannot pray prophetically, it is because we suppress it with our head.

Prophetic word for your heart:

"How long will you be blinded by the cares of this world? How long will you give attention to that which is temporal? My plans for you are eternal. I bring total fulfillment to your heart. I bring good news to you that you may soar through life even now."

Meditation-Prayer-Reflection
DAY FIVE

How did God speak to you today?

_____
_____
_____
_____
_____
_____
_____

What are your thoughts now?

___

How will you pray?

___

Day Six

Prophetic Prayers of the Heart, Part Two

Then the king said to Araunah, "No, but I will surely buy it from you for a price; nor will I offer burnt offerings to the Lord my God with that which costs me nothing.

2 Samuel 24:24a

David said to Araunah, "I will pay for this because I will not offer burnt offerings to the Lord that which costs me nothing." Prayer does cost us something. It can be pretty expensive at times. However, the cost of prayer is also a test of our hearts being surrendered to Christ. Real prayer is not produced in the natural, but in the spiritual realm. It is most effective when we are spiritually in tune with Christ as the head, the covering, and the flame of our prayers. He knows all that we should pray; He makes intercession on our behalf to help us in our infirmities. You will have difficulty in prayer when you do not depend upon the Holy Spirit to lead you through the prophetic pathway to prayer.

Romans 8:26-27 AMPC, reveals the need for the Holy Spirit in prophetic prayer. Your prophetic prayer life is to be a time of enjoyment and fulfillment; "So too, the [Holy] Spirit comes to our aid *and* bears us up in our weakness; for we do not know what prayer to offer *nor* how to offer it worthily as we ought, but the Spirit Himself goes to meet our supplication *and* pleads in our behalf with unspeakable yearnings *and* groanings too deep for utterance. And He Who searches the hearts of men knows what is in the mind of the [Holy] Spirit [what His intent is], because the Spirit intercedes *and* pleads [before God] on behalf of the saints according to *and* in harmony with God's will."

The most significant benefit of prayer is for us to be in the presence of the Lord, to hear from Him and be directed by Him. As we do this He is shaping and advancing our prophetic prayer life. The second most important part of prophetic prayer is to be changed. Knowledge by experience in fellowship with God is everything. Our daily encounter with the Lord is to be the most edifying experience of our life.

Prophetic words for your heart:

"My eyes can see, and My ears can hear the unspoken words of your heart. But do not fear nor be ashamed because of your weaknesses. I reach out to you all the time; I am here for you to pour out My love upon you. I am your freedom, your peace, and your strength; so, know Me."

Meditation-Prayer-Reflection
DAY SIX

How did God speak to you today?

_____

_____

_____

_____

_____

_____

_____

What are your thoughts now?

_____
_____
_____
_____
_____
_____

How will you pray?

_____
_____
_____

Day Seven

A Heart of Trust, Part One

Trust in the Lord with all your heart . . .
Proverbs 3:5a

Trust is a small word in letters but a very big word in life. Trust carries the meaning of believing in, having confidence in, secure in, dependability, stability and being reliable. Trust is a major part of our lives. You need trust to develop and build relationships, to depend on someone, to have a good marriage and to have fruitful relationships. Even when making major purchases, trust is required. Trust is at the root of your life when it comes to living a good and fruitful life. If you live always feeling uneasy, insecure, and inadequate about something or someone it's generally an issue of inner trust. Trust provides the needed security to make sound quality decisions. You need trust within yourself to live a fulfilling and quality life. We have to trust our doctor, our lawyer, and our pastor in order to keep them providing those needed services for us.

How do you develop a heart of trust and understanding? So often we have trust issues, and we struggle with understanding. Did you know that we were created by the Lord to be strong, faithful, and trusting vessels? We are made to be honorable, respectful, trustworthy, and effective people that are here to make a difference. Unfortunately, we have all experienced broken trust or had our trust violated or snatched from under us. This can put your guards up and cause you to become overly cautious and more suspicious. Trust is meant to be built and maintained. When there are trust issues, they create other issues and problems in life.

The need to have trust within self has never been more necessary and essential. Inner trust will give you freedom to make decisions, to move out in faith and to take risks. You must become a vessel with inner trust in order to live a life of freedom and peace.

Your prophetic word for your heart:

"Put the past behind you; set your face and focus on where I am ordering your steps. Yesterday is gone! Today I am with you to speak to you, to help you and to show you the way to go."

Meditation-Prayer-Reflection
DAY SEVEN

How did God speak to you today?

_____
_____
_____
_____
_____
_____
_____

What are your thoughts now?

_____
_____
_____
_____
_____
_____
_____

How will you pray?

_____
_____
_____

Day Eight

A Heart of Trust, Part Two

Trust in the Lord with all your heart . . .

Proverbs 3:5a

When you trust someone, you will open up to them more; you will listen to them increasingly and you will confide in them more. Real trust allows you to share innermost secrets with someone you love and have a close relationship. Trust makes life easier; it keeps you more at peace within yourself.

You are responsible for developing and building trust within yourself. You must begin to build that trust by laying the foundation for a deep, intimate, and sound relationship with the Lord. That union with the Lord begins with His word. As you hear the word of God, the Bible says that faith comes by hearing and hearing by the word of God. To build trust you must start with hearing God's word on a consistent basis. Then you must confess His word daily over and over again as a word in which you belive. You may even need to write down verses that speak to your heart and read them out loud over and over again.

You will also need to spend quality time in prayer in the presence of the Lord. You must talk to the Lord and also listen with expectation because you believe He has something to say to you. Your quality time with Him is so powerful. It will enrich your life. Your trust will develop faster, and you will get to know Him better. The more you get to know Him, the more you will find trust increasing. Your faith will get stronger; your confidence will grow, and you will become free. Your growth in the Lord will develop into growth in other areas. Now you can speak the word of faith and see amazing results revealed to you.

Prophetic word for your heart:

"My promises never fail; My words to you will never fall to the wayside. I am greater than your needs and I am bigger than your problems. As you walk today remember I will never leave you or forsake you. I have your future in My hand, and I will give you room to grow and expand to new heights and to new places. This is your day; a new normal for you to enjoy."

Meditation-Prayer-Reflection
DAY EIGHT

How did God speak to you today?

_____

_____

_____

_____

_____

_____

_____

What are your thoughts now?

_____

_____

_____

_____

_____

_____

_____

How will you pray?

_____

_____

_____

Day Nine

Do Not Lose Heart, Part One

For where your treasure is, there your heart will be also.

Matthew 6:21

The word heart here is the Greek word Cardiac meaning: thoughts, reasoning, understanding, emotions, affections and will. The word treasure has to do with wealth or something of great worth or value. It could be a collection of precious things or anything we place value in or hold dear. These could be such things as a home, jewels, money, marriage, or another person. Often, we talk about things of wealth in connection with natural or earthly things.

Have you ever lost heart? The phrase losing heart means: losing the nerves, the guts or the endurance to finish. Sometimes we allow ourselves to devalue our own selves and to quit or back up from moving forward.

II Corinthians 4:1-2,7 says: "Therefore, since we have this *ministry*, as we have *received* mercy, we do not lose heart. But we have *renounced* the hidden things of shame, not walking in craftiness nor handling the word of God deceitfully, but by manifestation of the truth commending ourselves to every man's conscience in the sight of God. But we have this treasure in earthen vessels that the excellence of the power may be of God and not of us."

So many people are losing heart today, giving up, throwing in the towel, living in constant chaos, confusion, and depression. Many are feeling so discouraged and overwhelmed with too many issues. We must remember the grace and the mercy of God which is able to give us the strength and the goodness of God. Jesus said, "You shall know the truth and the truth shall make you free." Remember goodness and mercy shall follow us all the days of our life.

You are unique, a designer's original, a vessel of class and purpose. You are not who your past says you are, and you are not a second-class citizen. You are a person of purpose, passion, and prestige. So, fill your heart by investing in new words of wisdom; surround yourself with people, understanding and influence.

Look for ways to do new things by stimulating new, creative ideas. Let these new creative ideas move you from the old to the new, from the past to the future and from failure to achievement. Your heart is waiting to be stretched outside of the limits of the old.

Prophetic Word for your heart today:

"Your road of recovery is not far off. I have planned and prepared great things for you. As I live so shall you live with Me; I have reserved long life for you. My word shall not fail you, but it shall make you and shape you into the image of My Son. Goodness and mercy are yours to enjoy.

Meditation-Prayer-Reflection

DAY NINE

How did God speak to you today?

_____

_____

_____
_____
_____
_____
_____
_____

What are your thoughts now?

_____
_____
_____
_____
_____

How will you pray?

_____
_____
_____

Day Ten

Do Not Lose Heart, Part Two

For where your treasure is, there your heart will be also.

Matthew 6:21

Your heart is to be the treasure of your life. It is to be that which blesses your life as a treasure and a valuable asset. Your heart is to bring you gain, increase, profit, and success. It is designed to make you happy, inspired and fulfilled. You are to live a life of great wealth and abundance. Your life is to be lived with great value, possessing the wonderful gifts of God. Most of all your life is to be filled with the very nature of God.

Your walk and relationship with the Lord are to make you a treasure. You and I were once unprofitable, unproductive, spiritually dead, and bankrupt. When Christ comes into our life we transfer out of darkness and into His marvelous light. We move from death to life, from loss to gain and from being at a disadvantage to having an advantage. Before Christ, our thoughts were negative, fearful, discouraging and occasionally depressing. In Christ, we live, move, and have our being in Him. You are now a new creature in Christ, the old things are passed away and new things have come.

When I first came to Christ, the old sin nature did not want to let go of me. It tried to keep me in the same old bondage of my past. The old nature would tell me that nothing had changed and that I was the same old person as before. However, the more that I heard the word, the more I began to see that faith comes by hearing and hearing by the word of God. I stayed under the word in spite of how I felt and in spite of my setbacks. I kept coming to be fed. The more of the word I heard the more I became stronger, more confident, and more determined about who I was in Christ.

That old, pathetic nature of darkness got weaker and weaker, and my spirit and soul got stronger, wiser, and better. I began to see the new me, feel the new me. My identity in Christ became my most valuable asset. The old nature of darkness must pass away because the new nature of light, life and truth has come. You are now a living treasure with loaded benefits in Christ.

Prophetic word for your heart:

"I hear the sound of the abundance of rain coming to you, to lift you up, to bless you and to prosper you. The latter-day rain is being poured out in great measure; so, stand in the rain, sit in the rain, pray in the rain, and taste and see that the Lord is good! The rain is coming to bring change to your life and to take you in a new direction."

Meditation-Prayer-Reflection
DAY TEN

How did God speak to you today?
_____
_____
_____
_____

What are your thoughts now?

How will you pray?

Day Eleven

We Rest, Part One

Trust in the Lord with all your heart . . .

Proverbs 3:5a

How well do you rest? I do not mean when you go to sleep, but rather how do you rest from toiling, from pressure and from anxiety. Rest is mentioned in scripture as a result of trusting in the Lord. Trust means to look to, to depend on, to believe in and to place your entire life in the security of the Lord. Rest means to cease from toiling, from self-efforts and from striving to survive. It is when we enter the place of trust in the Lord that we can rest. When the prosecutor completes his arguments on behalf of the state he says, "The people rest."

When your future, your present, your purpose, and your destiny is totally yielded to the nature of God, then you can rest. Just say, "I rest in You my Lord my redeemer." Rest comes when we feel confident, secure and at peace. Jesus said, "I will give you peace that surpasses all understanding." Our spiritual identity in Christ brings us into a place of rest, refuge, and assurance in Him.

Let's take a deeper look at certain scriptures to gain a greater, more divine understanding of its meaning. In Matthew 5:3 Jesus said, "Blessed are the poor in spirit for theirs is the Kingdom of heaven." This verse addresses five main areas of your spirit and soul in relation to you and God:

a. Your deepest and most intimate focus is on God

b. Absolute and complete surrender to God

c. Releasing a self-willed lifestyle over to Christ

d. Self-denial giving up our own desires e.

Trusting in Christ in all things

Your Prophetic word for your heart today:

"I am the same yesterday, today and forever. I AM your today and your tomorrow. I see you as the apple of My eye and My reward is with Me. I have not forgotten about you even when you lost focus and turned from Me. I am here to love you, to carry you through your destiny of life. I have proven Myself to you; believe that I have your welfare and your future in My heart."

Meditation-Prayer-Reflection
DAY ELEVEN

How did God speak to you today?

_____
_____
_____
_____
_____
_____
_____

What are your thoughts now?

_____
_____
_____
_____
_____
_____
_____

How will you pray?

_____
_____
_____
_____

Day Twelve

We Rest, Part Two

Trust in the Lord with all your heart . . .

Proverbs 3:5a

Trusting in the Lord is for our benefit; it places us in a spiritual position where the Lord is able to keep our focus on Him. Staying focused on Him and finding our habitation in Him is where we rest. If everything has to go our way and we have to be in control, then we do not fully trust Him. We have not found rest. Rest is a condition of the heart and of the mind where both have surrendered and stopped toiling. There is a place in our walk and talk with the Lord where we find Christ and make the full transfer over to Him. This is when we release all and look for everything to be found in Him.

He tells us to abide in Him. In John 15:5-7 AMPC, the scripture says, "I am the Vine; you are the branches. Whoever lives in Me and I in him bears much (abundant) fruit. However, apart from Me [cut off from vital union with Me] you can do nothing. If a person does not dwell in Me, he is thrown out like a [broken-off] branch, and withers; such branches are gathered up and thrown into the fire, and they are burned. If you live in Me [abide vitally united to Me] and My words remain in you and continue to live in your hearts, ask whatever you will, and it shall be done for you."

Rest comes from moving from a visitation lifestyle with Christ to a habitation lifestyle. It is when we truly live in Him that His life will manifest in us. Christ waits till the old us stops wrestling and struggling within us. He will not fight for position or authority. He already has complete authority, so He is not trying to take anything from us. We rest as we are in complete harmony with Him. We are to live this new life seeing ourselves as spiritually, upgraded people that have found our spiritual place, position, and lifestyle in Christ.

Prophetic word for your Heart:

"Better days are coming to you. You will know that I the Lord am bringing you into a new place that you have never been before. I require new steps, new prayers, and new thoughts. I have done a new thing in you, so walk before Me in newness of life. I am waiting on your arrival."

Meditation-Prayer-Reflection
DAY TWELVE

How did God speak to you today?

_____

_____

_____

_____

_____

_____

_____

What are your thoughts now?

_____
_____
_____
_____
_____
_____

How will you pray?

_____
_____
_____

Day Thirteen

Healing From A Broken Heart, Part One

He has sent Me to heal the brokenhearted . . .

Luke 4:18d

Have you ever had a broken heart? Do you know how it feels? How do you recover from a broken heart? If you are 30 years of age or older you have probably experienced a broken heart. The scripture shows us that the Lord is concerned about people with a broken heart, "The LORD is near to the brokenhearted and saves the crushed in spirit (Psalms 34:18)." It is encouraging to read what King David wrote. We can be healed and delivered from a broken heart!

A broken heart can occur when we suffer the loss of one such as a spouse, a child or even a beloved pet. Metaphorically it is that emotional aching in your chest that happens when you are deeply disappointed or grieved over a life circumstance. The Bible has many other verses that can encourage the brokenhearted as well.

Psalms 73:26, "My flesh and my heart may fail, but God is the strength of my heart and my portion forever."

Isaiah 41:10, "Fear not, for I am with you; be not dismayed, for I am your God; I will strengthen you, I will help you, I will uphold you with my righteous right hand."

Matthew 11:28-30, "Come to me, all who labor and are heavy laden, and I will give you rest. Take my yoke upon you, and learn from me, for I am gentle and lowly in heart, and you will find rest for your souls. For my yoke is easy, and my burden is light."

John 14:27, "Peace I leave with you; my peace I give to you. Not as the world gives do I give to you. Let not your hearts be troubled, neither let them be afraid."

Prophetic Prayer and Prophecy:

"Lord, I pray that you will heal me from a broken heart. May You console me and refresh my soul. I need a touch from You, and I need You to make me whole and deliver me from the longing pain of grief."

"Fear not My child I am with you. I am your breakthrough and your promise keeper. I will heal you from the griefs and despairs of this world. Hold on and I will take you with Me to new places that you have never known."

Meditation-Prayer-Reflection
DAY THIRTEEN

How did God speak to you today?

_____
_____
_____
_____
_____
_____
_____

What are your thoughts now?

_____

_____

_____

_____

_____

_____

How will you pray?

_____

_____

_____

_____

Day Fourteen

Healing From A Broken Heart, Part Two

He has sent Me to heal the brokenhearted . . .

Luke 4:18d

How do you know when you have a broken heart? A broken heart can be quite severe and very painful. It can be traumatic, extremely uncomfortable, and lingering. Most broken hearts come from relational issues such as a broken relationship, divorce, or the loss of a loved one. Broken heartedness can also come from a major loss in life, failure, or severe rejection.

A broken heart can cause extreme anxiety, serious pressure, discouragement, and depression. A broken-hearted person can become overly sensitive, hopeless, insecure, and over reactive. When people are in a broken-hearted state of mind, they do not think and can be very vulnerable. Broken hearted people are wounded people that carry the pain of their wounds in their heart. This can cause restlessness, sleepless nights, a loss of appetite and extreme fatigue. The healing process of a broken heart is:

Do not spend a lot of time alone

Get wise counsel or some mature person with whom to talk

Share your pain and your thoughts with the right person

Press your way to hear the word of God often

Find activities and functions to attend

Read scripture regarding comfort, peace, and freedom

Pray constantly and participate in prayer meetings

Stay in contact with someone when you are alone

Do not make quick decisions

Do not engage too quickly with the opposite sex

Stay active, involved, and serve others

Read books, listen to CD's and positive audio

Prophetic words for your heart:

"Your name is heard in My ears says the Lord! I will call you and speak words of life to you. I am the breath of life, I am your refuge, I am your peace, and I am your strength. All that trust in Me shall see My ways and My works shall be manifested within you.

I will bring you fresh flowers; I will blow fresh winds of tender whispers that will tell of My love for you and how I have kept you alive. Live!"

Meditation-Prayer-Reflection
DAY FOURTEEN

How did God speak to you today?

_____

_____

_____

_____

_____
_____
_____
_____

What are your thoughts now?

_____
_____
_____
_____
_____
_____

How will you pray?

_____
_____
_____
_____

Day Fifteen
The Peace That Guards Your Hearts, Part One

. . . and the peace of God, which surpasses all understanding, will guard your hearts and minds through Christ Jesus.

Philippians 4:7

I grew up in a home with lots of brothers and sisters. I have six sisters and four brothers for a total of 11 children. My mom was always home, but my dad was seldom around. We also had too many children and too small of a house. We never had enough bedrooms or beds. I always had to sleep with one of my brothers and I always had to rock them to sleep. When I rocked, my brother and I got sleepy. He would often say, "I'm not sleep yet and I would get punched. So, after he would finally go to sleep it seemed that I would be wide awake.

I had a difficult time trying to get to sleep because I would hear strange noises and I would see things in the dark. Sometimes I thought that I even felt something touch me. I was a very fearful child. I was terrorized in the night because of the spooky feelings I had and the bad dreams that tormented me. I would wake up my brothers many nights because I either heard something, saw something, or felt something. My fear was out of control. I believed in ghosts and all types of things.

I did not get delivered from fear until I got saved and trusted in the Lord. I love the word of God because it is really truth that works. Philippians 4:6-7 says, "Do not be anxious about anything, but in everything, by prayer and petition, with thanksgiving, present your requests to God. And the peace of God, which transcends all understanding, will guard your hearts and your minds in Christ Jesus." This scripture tells us not to worry about anything, but in everything by prayer and petitions, with thanksgiving to present our request unto God. Are you struggling with worry, fear, doubt, or confusion? Then my question to you is, "How is your prayer life?" I am not talking about just talking to God with many words. Prayer has to be intimate, passionate, and relational in order for it to be effective.

Prophetic Words for the heart:

"I have food for you that you do not know of; I will feed you faith food. You shall know that I am Your necessary provisions. Your peace and your joy come from Me. You shall know that I am with you, and I will never leave you."

Meditation-Prayer-Reflection
DAY FIFTEEN

How did God speak to you today?

_____

_____

_____

_____

_____

What are your thoughts now?

How will you pray?

Day Sixteen

The Peace That Guards Your Hearts, Part Two

. . . and the peace of God, which surpasses all understanding, will guard your hearts and minds through Christ Jesus.
Philippians 4:7

I grew up without peace and tormented. My fears were completely developed. My childhood was full of darkness that kept me afraid. Fear has the ability to bind you up, control you with thoughts of demonic oppression. I did not know anything about demons or devils, but I knew that evil was out there because I felt it and heard it. If only in my mind, it was there.

Parents do not ignore your children when they tell you that something is in their room or that something touched them. The enemy has a way of really tormenting children. He will use anything he can to torture them. Fear comes in through sin, ignorance, bad experiences, through an ungodly atmosphere and demonic activity. The Bible says that fear brings torment. The enemy specializes in fear, but God specializes in love and peace.

How do we overcome fear and torment? The Bible says, "For God has not given us a spirit of fear, but of power and of love and of a sound mind (2 Timothy 1:7)." The closer we draw to the Lord, the freer we become from fear and anxiety. The way that we get delivered from fear is to first pray about everything. That means we must take everything to God in genuine, heartfelt prayer. Then we must spend quality time just giving thanks to God as a confident sign that we believe in Him. Tell Him how appreciative we are and how much we need Him. Release your requests and desires before Him. Now wait and let God flood you with His peace that surpasses all understanding. This means that His peace will be out of this world, and it will come in spite of all the thoughts and concerns around you. God surpasses everything!

Prophetic word for your heart:

"In a world of great shame, guilt and despair remember Me, that I the Lord your God have delivered you and ransomed you from all of your enemies. I have paid in full for all guilt and shame; I have given you a new beginning and a fresh start. Today I have called you by name, I have spoken well of you and given you a new name. My plans for you have not changed; they are good, full of My love, peace, and joy."

Meditation-Prayer-Reflection

DAY SIXTEEN

How did God speak to you today?

_____
_____
_____
_____
_____
_____
_____

What are your thoughts now?

_____

_____

_____

_____

_____

_____

How will you pray?

_____

_____

_____

Day Seventeen

Don't Give Up Today

Now the purpose of the commandment is love from a pure heart, from good conscience, and from sincere faith . . .

I Timothy 1:5

You may be facing challenges, difficulties, and uncomfortable times in your life. You may be facing heart brokenness and dismay through some extremely tough circumstances.

What are you up against? What is working against you today? The scripture says in Ecclesiastes 9:3, "This evil is in all that is done under the sun: one fate comes to all. Also, the hearts of men are full of evil, and madness is in their hearts while they live and after they go to the dead."

This scripture reveals that there is an inner evil on the inside of our hearts that wants to work against us all the time. This can be very disturbing, discouraging and depressing. However, there is good news on the inside of you and you didn't put it there by any of your own efforts. The best thing is that you have accepted God into your heart, and He has responded in a really big way.

David said to the Lord in Psalm 51:10 AMPC, "Create in me a clean heart, O God, and renew a right, preserving and steadfast spirit within me."

Your prayer to God awakens the excellence of God within you. A clean heart comes from the Lord; it comes from His very nature, His character and DNA. Your call for a clean heart will reveal the purity and righteousness of the heart of God within you. You are closer than you think towards a clean heart. The only thing lacking is for you to believe.

Your prophetic word for your heart today:

"Be sure when you come to Me; know what is in your heart. When you come to Me, come in the boldness and confidence of Me, with all your heart. As you come let your heart be full of the wisdom of My words. Come up My child. Let Me show you the glory of My Kingdom and the power in My name. In your weakness I will reveal My strength to you. You shall know Me as a child knows his father. Come taste and see that My goodness will be poured out upon you today."

Meditation-Prayer-Reflection

DAY SEVENTEEN

How did God speak to you today?

_____
_____
_____
_____
_____
_____
_____

What are your thoughts now?

_____

_____

_____

_____

_____

_____

How will you pray?

_____

_____

_____

_____

Day Eighteen

Walk With A Pure Heart

For assuredly, I say to you, whoever says to this mountain, "Be removed and be cast into the sea," and does not doubt in his heart, but believes that those things he says will be done, he will have whatever he says.

Mark 11:23

Do you feel like your heart is not so pure even though you are born-again, and Spirit filled? Well don't condemn yourself and assume that you are unsaved. The scripture tells us in Jeremiah 17:9 AMPC, "The heart is deceitful above all things, it is exceedingly perverse and corrupt and severely, mortally sick! Who can understand, be acquainted with his own heart and mind? I the Lord search the mind; I try the heart, even to give to every man according to his ways, according to the fruit of his doings." When you feel evil thoughts and emotions rising within you, just remember that verse. So often we don't know why we feel certain ways or why certain thoughts just seem to flood our minds for no reason at all. Sometimes you just feel out of control with rage, anger, lust or even thoughts of murder. These are thoughts of the heart that come from the enemy in our old nature. You are not this terrible person consumed by this ungodly evil without hope or help from God.

You have a purpose and an identity from your heavenly Father. His will and plan for your life is to give you His heart of righteousness, love, peace, and purity. This means that God's ultimate goal and purpose for your life is the charge of love which comes from God because He is love. His very nature and attribute is love. You must claim your new identity from your heavenly.

Father as a child of God. Remember, you have your Father's DNA and attributes. You must confess your new life. There is no shame in realizing that the old nature will fight against you, but you must fight back in your new nature. Choose to fight back with the strongest power available to the heart and that is the power of love.

Prophetic word for your heart today:

"I have seen, heard, and known you in the most intimate details of your life. I know you by name. I have prepared a way of life for you that you may live and not die. I have waited for you to grow up and blossom as a fresh, tender flower. I have fixed your eyes to focus on Me that you may see Me in the deepest way. My way is preserved for you. I have anointed your eyes with oil that you may clearly see the way prepared for you."

Meditation-Prayer-Reflection

DAY EIGHTEEN

How did God speak to you today?

_____

_____

_____

_____

_____

_____

What are your thoughts now?

How will you pray?

Day Nineteen
No Doubt In My Heart, Part One

For assuredly, I say to you, whoever says to this mountain, "Be removed and be cast into the sea," and does not doubt in his heart, but believes that those things he says will be done, he will have whatever he says.

Mark 11:23

I can remember growing up as a child and imaging myself doing many, big things. I wished for certain things, and I would see myself getting what I wanted, and it would happen. Even though I did know the Lord, I had a type of faith and belief that I could see things change. I did not really understand what was happening, but I felt good about how things turned out. Looking back now, I believe that God was dealing with my heart at an early age, even though I did not surrender to Him until I was 29 years old.

Jesus said, "I assure you that you can say to this mountain, 'May God lift you up and throw you into the sea,' and your command will be obeyed. All that's required is that you really believe and do not doubt in your heart. Listen to me! You can pray for anything, and if you believe, you will have it." Mark 11:23-24 AMPC.

What are the mountains in your life? Yes, I said mountains because each of us have more than one thing that is like a mountain to us. A mountain represents something huge, something hard, tough and something deeply grounded and planted with a strong foundation. Mountains can be a stronghold such as sickness, poverty, broken relationships, debts, guilt, and shame, etc. Mountains are mainly strongholds that have been around a long time. They seem to be impossible to move or to remove. I know what the mountains of my life have been, but do you know your mountains?

Based upon this scripture, we learn that mountains can be removed or moved. Your heart is the most important part of moving mountains out of the way. It all starts with your heart being developed in faith based upon the word of God. We must move from church minded thinking to kingdom believing and living.

Prophetic word for your heart:

"I look for the reflection of Myself within your heart. When I see Myself within you then I can show you yourself. I, even I will do marvelous things for you. I will show Myself strong and I will make you into another man."

Meditation-Prayer-Reflection
DAY NINETEEN

How did God speak to you today?

_____
_____
_____
_____

What are your thoughts now?

How will you pray?

Day Twenty

No Doubt In My Heart, Part Two

For assuredly, I say to you, whoever says to this mountain, "Be removed and be cast into the sea," and does not doubt in his heart, but believes that those things he says will be done, he will have whatever he says.

Mark 11:23

The fears in my life were based upon my feeling of helplessness, hopelessness, insecurity, inadequacy, and inferiority. My mind was fear based and operated from a disadvantaged standpoint. As long as I allowed myself to think this way, it was like seeing a big wall that was immovable which I could not get pass. The mountain in your life represents something that has probably been defeating you all of your life; for you it is an immovable mountain.

There was a church building located at 901 W. 47th Avenue in Gary, Indiana. We were currently holding services at 2500 W. 11th Avenue. I would pass this new location all the time. I said to myself, "I would love to be in that church building." However, I also said, "That property would never be for sale." Then one day I passed by it, and it was up for sale. I got so excited because it was like a dream come true. Well, we only had a few people with us, and the seller wanted two hundred thousand dollars with forty thousand dollars down. So, to add it all up, it seemed like a million dollars.

I saw pass that mountain, pass the two hundred thousand dollars and pass the forty thousand dollars down. But how this would happen I did not know. I shared the vision with the body, and they embraced it, rejoiced, and went to work. I saw the mountain moved and they saw the mountain moved. We ran into several obstacles, but we were focused, determined and passionate. We saw every obstacle moved out of the way. Our faith was alive and well; we spoke to our mountains every day and spoke life to our situation.

What is your mountain and where is your faith today? You must first believe that every mountain is removable. Again, every mountain is removable! Now you must believe, see and say! Believe that God is able, see the mountain removed or moved and speak it as a daily confession.

Prophetic word for your heart:

"I, the Lord, have given you all that you need, only believe. You have rights in heaven that are greater than your ills on the earth. I have given you all that you need so use your faith and release My abundant blessings."

Meditation-Prayer-Reflection

DAY TWENTY

How did God speak to you today?

_____

_____

_____

_____

What are your thoughts now?

How will you pray?

Day Twenty-One

Hope Deferred

Hope deferred makes the heart sick, but when desire comes it is a tree of life.

Proverbs 13:12

Have you ever wanted something so very bad, but did not get it? Have you ever worked so hard to do something, but did not accomplish it? Have you ever procrastinated about taking care of something and ended up suffering the consequences? Each of these examples can be described as hope deferred.

The word hope means confident expectation. It can give you a sure feeling that something will work out. Hope is a type of desire for something, meaning that it's in your sight. It seems to be in view, and you have a good feeling that it can be obtain. Hope is connected to faith, but it's the first phase of faith, it's getting those expected juices flowing. When you hope, you have triggered desire and the power of seeing it, tasting it, and receiving it have been activated. Hope puts you and your heart in motion, but faith takes action to bring it to pass.

Hope deferred is when that which you expected is late, delayed, postponed, or cancelled. There are many things in this life that you cannot have, even though you ask for, pray for, or even work for them. There is the forbidden fruit, meaning something you really, really want, but is not for you. Sometimes our desires are premature and it's not yet time for it to be received. Hope deferred can be a God thing to protect you from your own desire.

So often, when you experience too many delays through failure, false starts, unrealistic expectations, or someone not coming through a heart sickness is created. When someone just lied and did not tell you the truth, it can create a heart sickness. The word sick comes from the word disease. When life happens, it can leave you in depression and despair.

You want to do all that you can to focus on real based upon what is reserved for you. You never want to have false hope. False hope comes from not having real faith for it because it was based on what someone else had. This false hope can also be based on selfishness, greed, covetousness or just to prove that you could possess such a thing.

Prophetic prayer:

Lord, I pray that You will help me to desire only those things that are reserved for me. I pray that I will have a pure heart and a realistic hope from you. Greater is He that is in me than he that is in the world.

Meditation-Prayer-Reflection

DAY TWENTY-ONE

How did God speak to you today?

_____

_____

_____

What are your thoughts now?

How will you pray?

Day Twenty-Two
Desire

Hope deferred makes the heart sick, but when desire comes it is a tree of life.

Proverbs 13:12

The word desire can be inclinations, pleasures, imaginations, visions, or anything you see as enticing. Desire can be good, or it can be bad. An example is to desire sweets so much that you crave them, which can lead to a sugar addiction. So not all desires are good for you even though you want them. But there are some very good desires that are even pleasing and acceptable to God.

Psalm 37:4 says, "Commit yourself also to the Lord and He will give you the desires of your heart." This scripture confirms Proverbs 12:13b "But when desire is fulfilled, it is a tree of life."

So how do we inherit or obtain good desires? The scripture tells us to commit ourselves to the Lord. The word commit is making an unwavering, stable, and sound vow from the heart to Him. This type of commitment is even sacrificial, sure, and loyal. When we commit to the Lord our first priority and focus is to please Him. In pleasing Him, we also want to honor Him. An example in scripture in Matthew 6:33, "But seek first the Kingdom of God and His righteousness." When we are committed to the Lord, we will put Him first. The order is just as important as the deed.

When God is first and our yearning to please Him is rooted and grounded in our heart, then real desire can be fulfilled. As the scripture says, "When desire is fulfilled it is a tree of life." A tree of life represents strength, growth, development, fruitfulness, and stability. God wants to give us the desires of our hearts, but he wants us to have good desires that will prosper, bless our lives, and make us fruitful.

Prophetic word for your heart:

"Today I give you new dreams, new visions, and new expectations. I am the Lord your promise keeper, you're exceeding and great reward. I have more for you, even beyond your imagination. You shall see what was not there before. I will plant new thoughts and give you a new beginning because I love you."

Meditation-Prayer-Reflection

DAY TWENTY-TWO

How did God speak to you today?

_____

_____

_____

_____

_____

_____

_____

What are your thoughts now?

___

___

___

___

___

___

How will you pray?

___

___

___

___

Day Twenty-Three

Final Is Not Final, Part One

God is Spirit, and those who worship Him must worship in spirit and truth.

John 4:24

Have you ever experienced what we call failure? Well, it happens to us all and sometimes we seem to fail in the same area over and over again. The painful thing about it is that it makes you feel less than adequate, ignorant, disqualified, unacceptable and incapable. The enemy and our emotions have a way of making us feel very low, insecure, and dumb . . . to put it bluntly. But is that really the truth or is there something about our life which are just necessary steps that must be taken . . . even failures?

In the book of John, chapter 4, there was a woman that met Jesus at the well to get water. Several amazing things began to happen. When she got there, Jesus was sitting and resting by the well. It was around noon when the woman arrived. This was her routine in order to try to avoid seeing and being ridiculed by the other women. However, to her surprise Jesus, a Jew, was there at that time. The first amazing thing that happened was the fact the He spoke to her. Jews did not speak to Samaritans because they were considered the rejects of society, the low life people of His day. Yet totally contrary to the custom of the Jewish people, he actually spoke to her. He actually asked her for a drink.

You may be facing some of the most difficult times of your life and have begun to isolate yourself. You may be carrying all the signs of a failure and experiencing the rejection of man. You may be in a time of despair, frustration and maybe even desperation.

This woman had given up on what she believed and had dropped her morals. Her belief system had been crushed and now she had wavered from her faith and confidence in God.

Prophetic Word for your heart:

"I have plans for you that you know not of. I have always seen your heart and it still has the treasures that I released in it. I have prepared you for such a time as this and you are not alone. Did I not tell you that perfect love has no fear? So, fear not My child for I am with you and My blessings for you will not fail. Look to Me with all your heart and see Me in ways you have not known!"

Meditation-Prayer-Reflection
DAY TWENTY-THREE

How did God speak to you today?
_____
_____
_____
_____
_____
_____
_____

What are your thoughts now?

___

___

___

___

___

___

___

How will you pray?

___

___

___

___

Day Twenty-Four

Final Is Not Final, Part Two

God is Spirit, and those who worship Him must worship in spirit and truth.

John 4:24

The woman at the well had settled in her heart that she had to accept whatever she could get out of life. She no longer believed that she was worthy of marriage. To her, marriage was for some people, but no longer for her. Failure has a way of making you reject yourself and it dilutes your purpose in life. You have a tendency of disqualifying yourself—but stop it! *Yes, I said Stop It Right Now!*

Alert! Alert! Jesus is coming to meet you at the well, the well of your heart despair and pain! You will encounter a visitor that will not come to ridicule you, but to bless you. He will come to reach out to you, to accept you and never reject you.

Jesus had asked the woman to give Him a drink, but she was in shock and couldn't believe that He was speaking to her. So, she asked, "How is it that You being a Jew are asking me a Samaritan for a drink?" Wow! This was unheard of and a shocking surprise. The other Samaritans were not even talking to her. Yet here the King of Kings, Lord of Lords and the Savoir of the world was taking the time to talk to her. Not only talking to her, but He asked her to give Him something. What can we give to God who has everything?

In spite of what we have done, He will . . . In spite of what we think He will . . . In spite of how others think of us and far beyond the traditions, customs, and the way the community around us believes, *God will come!* He comes reaching out to us, He comes bearing gifts, and He comes with answers to heal our broken heart.

Prophetic words for your heart:

"Who says you can't, who says you won't? I am the Lord your God and I say yes to your dreams, yes to your visions, yes to your calling, yes to your destiny and yes you are forgiven. I say, forgive yourself and be free to fulfill your divine destiny. I have chosen you when others rejected you, hated or despised you. Shut out the words against you; listen and I will speak words of life to you says the Living God!"

Meditation-Prayer-Reflection

DAY TWENTY- FOUR

How did God speak to you today?

_____
_____
_____
_____
_____
_____

What are your thoughts now?

_____
_____
_____
_____
_____
_____

How will you pray?

_____
_____
_____
_____

Day Twenty-Five

Harden Not Your Heart, Part One

Do not harden your hearts, as in the rebellion, as in the day of]trial in the wilderness . . .

Psalm 95:8

Have you ever heard the saying or read the scripture "Do not harden your heart?" This phrase lets us know that we can harden our heart. So now we need to understand what that really means. To harden your heart means that we have either entered into a state of rebellion or we have shut down and are no longer open, transparent, or receptive. Sometimes we think that we can shut down on people and still be open to God. This is where we miss it or get it twisted. Let's say you grew up as a child with some very bad experiences with your parents and they were at fault. You may have suffered abuse, rejection and severe trust issues that left you hating your parents and feeling like they violated your trust and security. Because they represented authority, leadership, and parental security to you, it can cause you to automatically feel threatened by all other authority figures and leadership. It also can very easily cause you to have a hardened heart.

A hardened heart can cause Immense rebellion against all authority in your life. Rebellion is putting up a defense and resistance to the authority assigned to you. When you rebel, you are entering a state of defensiveness and rejection. You take an opposing position against them and against all that they say and request of you. Rebellion can cause you to revolt against all authority, including God's authority. It is a sign of a hardened heart. This can create distrust, dishonor, disrespect, and dissention. You can live a life of deception, not realizing that you are really in rebellion because rebellion can also create denial.

You must start by openly confessing before the Lord that you have hardened your heart, then ask the Lord to forgive you and help you.

Prophetic word for your heart:

"I have spoken to you in times past and I speak now to your heart that My love for you is eternal and everlasting. My love covers a multitude of sins. I give you a new heart and a new life. I say live! Live the life that I paid for you to enjoy.

Meditation-Prayer-Reflection
DAY TWENTY- FIVE

How did God speak to you today?

_____
_____
_____
_____
_____
_____

What are your thoughts now?

___

How will you pray?

___

Day Twenty-Six

Harden Not Your Heart, Part Two

Do not harden your hearts, as in the rebellion, as in the day of trial in the wilderness . . .

Psalm 95:8

I had a relatively good life as a child. I had lots of brothers and sisters and we all got along well. I was number four among the total eleven siblings. We laughed a lot and we played together. We really had good relationships as children. I share that because I do not know what it must feel like to be abused by parents or siblings, or to have a sibling that murdered another sibling. I do not know what it's like to grow up in a household where everyone hates one another.

I must confess one deep issue that I did have with my father. I felt like I could not do anything right in his eyes, no matter how hard I tried to please him. I felt like he picked on me and that he did not want to see me enjoy myself with my friends. I must admit, I thought about his truck blowing up with him in it on numerous occasions. Now those were only childhood thoughts. I did not understand why I was treated unfairly from my perspective. By God's grace I grew up with no serious issues like becoming a mass murderer, a child abuser, a sex offender, or other such thing.

God has a master plan to help us deal with all sorts of issues, no matter how bad. He is able to heal. A heart that has been seriously wounded can easily become hardened. Maybe you have one and do not know it. Maybe you are threatened by authority figures and those that tell you what to do. Consider this, maybe your heart has become cynical. Just bow your head and tell God "I may have a hardened heart and I need your help Lord to be healed." You have begun the process for your healing and restoration. Now find someone you trust to pray with you and to mentor you to full recovery.

Prophetic word for your heart:

See I have given you life and life more abundantly. So, choose life and live the free life that never dies and never grows old. You shall live and declare the works of the Lord. Have I not shown you what is good? I will heal your broken heart.

Meditation-Prayer-Reflection
DAY TWENTY- SIX

How did God speak to you today?
_____
_____
_____
_____
_____
_____
_____

What are your thoughts now?

How will you pray?

Day Twenty-Seven

The Worshiper In You, Part One

God is Spirit, and those who worship Him must worship in spirit and truth.

John 4:24

Did you know that there is a worshipper on the inside of you? In spite of what you might think of yourself, there is a true worshipper on the inside of you. Worship is the act of yielding, surrendering, submitting, and coming under the authority, rule, and glory of God. When we worship, we are actually surrendering our thoughts, desires, plans and will to the Lord.

We learn something amazing from the woman at the well to whom Jesus talked. When everyone else stayed away from her, rejected her, condemned her, and talked about her, Jesus, the Holy Son of God reached out to her. He talked with her and asked her to give Him some water. He also told her to go and get her husband, but she said to Him, "I have no husband." That must have been painful especially when He said to her, "You have had five husbands." Wow! What pain and hurt must have surfaced in her heart hearing those words from Jesus. How would you feel if you were asked to get your husband and you said, "I do not have one of those?" Your heart would drop if He said that you had five husbands or five wives. That had to bring back some bad memories that were very painful.

After all that, the woman brought up the well saying that our father Jacob drew water and worshipped at this well. Jesus quickly responded and told her that she really didn't understand and that the Jews were called to worship God. Then He told her that the Father was seeking worshippers. He is not seeking religious people, not just scripture quoting, not new members, but true worshippers to worship the Father in spirit and in truth. You will not find any higher requirement or any higher position than to be a true worshipper of God. Are you a true worshipper of God? The hallmark of a true Christian is to be a true worshipper of God.

Prophetic word for your heart:

Despise not your life or where you are today. I have called you unto Myself, so come to Me though you are tired and weary, I say come! You have seen Me afar off, so now come closer and get to know Me and get to know My ways. My ways are better, My gifts are better, My love is better, My plans are better, and My provisions are better. I am waiting!

Meditation-Prayer-Reflection
DAY TWENTY- SEVEN

How did God speak to you today?

_____

_____

_____

_____

_____

_____

_____

What are your thoughts now?

_____
_____
_____
_____
_____
_____
_____

How will you pray?

_____
_____
_____
_____

Day Twenty-Eight

The Worshiper In You, Part Two

God is Spirit, and those who worship Him must worship in spirit and truth.

John 4:24

Jesus said, "a time will come, however, indeed it is already here, when the true (genuine) worshippers will worship the Father in spirit and in truth (reality); the Father is seeking just such people as these as His worshipers (John 4:23 AMPC)."

This statement made by Jesus is the real key, root, and foundation to true Christianity. All that Jesus did on the cross of Calvary was to raise up true worshippers. Let us not forget that Jesus was talking with a woman that was not a Jew. She was not living for God, she was shacking, and her life was in a big mess. So, what is your excuse? Your life may be in a real mess. You may be struggling with moral issues, failure issues, relationship issues, truth issues or character issues. He will still come to you and reach out to you and share His living water with you. He is looking for people that everyone else has given up on and maybe they have given up on themselves.

He is seeking and searching for worshippers that will worship Him in spirit and in truth. Like the woman at the well, even though her life was in a mess, Jesus had a message for her. Your life may be in a mess, and you may feel like no one cares about you. You are the perfect candidate. You need to know that Jesus cares about everything that concerns you. You are a hidden worshipper, you have been concealed, but Jesus knows who you are, and He sees you just as you live. You are a worshipper unknown and hidden, but your heart is seen and known by the Lord. He has living water to share with you so that He can reveal the real you. When the woman at the well found out that she was a worshipper now revealed, she left the water bucket. She ran to openly share her new testimony with her people. Are you ready to share that you are a worshipper of Jesus?

Prophetic word for your heart:

"Look and see I have provided for you. There is no more shame and no more wickedness to battle with. I am the Way, the Truth and the Life and I have life to exchange with you for the death that holds you down. I am your exceeding and great reward so bow down and worship Me."

Meditation-Prayer-Reflection

DAY TWENTY- EIGHT

How did God speak to you today?

_____
_____
_____
_____
_____
_____
_____

What are your thoughts now?

_____

_____

_____

_____

_____

_____

_____

How will you pray?

_____

_____

_____

_____

Day Twenty-Nine
A Heart Filled With The Voice Of God, Part One

Therefore, behold, I will allure her, Will bring her into the wilderness, And speak comfort to her.

Hosea 2:14

There is nothing like the voice of God. But better than that, is for you to be a carrier of the voice of God. Can you imagine there are people who love the Lord and do not believe He speaks to them? They have hope and faith in Him but still do not believe that He speaks to them. Now that is so hard for me to understand, because our God is so relational. He has authored sixty-six books called the Bible that confirm He speaks to man. But there is even one issue better than His authorship of sixty-six books. You are to be a carrier of the voice of God.

I can remember the first time I heard the voice of God in a strong, clear way. I had gone to Liberty Temple for the first time for a noon service. I left there feeling so refreshed, renewed, and freed. I called my wife and told her what had happened and how we needed to fast and pray that night. When I got home, we got on our knees and got into the presence of the Lord. We felt the power of His presence so quickly. The voice of the Lord came suddenly with great boldness. His presence was so real to me that I felt a strong, personal presence as if the Lord was standing over me. His voice came forth with extreme directness and kingdom authority. He said, "Humble yourselves in My presence." I felt like He was talking directly to me. I curled up even more in a deeper degree of humility. Then He said, "I command you to love one another." Those words were like a shock wave to my heart and soul. This was the strongest, deepest presence of God and the clearest that I have ever heard His voice. It impacted my life for many years to come.

Hearing the voice of God is one of the most important experiences of your life other than salvation. Purpose yourself to focus on hearing His voice. Your life and prosperity depend on hearing from Him. One word from God can catapult your destiny onto orbit.

Prophetic word for your heart:

I will change your words as I change your heart; give Me your heart and make room for Me. I have made room for you, so let Me show you; let Me stretch you into another person. My ways are higher, and My words are higher than the earth. There is more, so much more for you to see, hear and do, so much more from Me.

Meditation-Prayer-Reflection

DAY TWENTY- NINE

How did God speak to you today?

_____
_____
_____
_____
_____

_____

_____

What are your thoughts now?

_____

_____

_____

_____

_____

_____

How will you pray?

_____

_____

_____

_____

Day Thirty

A Heart Filled With The Voice Of God, Part Two

Therefore, behold, I will allure her, Will bring her into the wilderness, And speak comfort to her.

Hosea 2:14

When was the last time you heard the voice of God for yourself? When did He speak and what did He say? How do you know that it was the Lord speaking to you? When He did speak how did you respond to His voice? How did His voice sound? Does He speak to you often? These are a few questions that are important for you to answer. You should be excited to talk about your experiences of hearing from the Lord.

Did you know that God has always spoken to His people? He will always continue to speak to us because He is a loving and relational Father? Hebrews 1:1-2 NLT says, "Long ago God spoke many times and in many ways to our ancestors through the prophets. And now in these final days, he has spoken to us through his Son. God promised everything to the Son as an inheritance, and through the Son he created the universe." Isn't that just awesome to know, that He has always spoken many times and in many ways? This means that He does not just speak every fifty, twenty or ten years, but He speaks all the time. Secondly, He has spoken to us through His Son. This takes me to His word and His works that were done through Christ and read about in the scriptures. It tells me the Son of God is speaking to us now through the Holy Spirit within us. He has much to say to us and His words are always life changing.

Hosea 2:14-16 AMPC, "Therefore, behold, I will allure her, (Israel) and bring her into the wilderness, and I will speak tenderly and to her heart." Maybe you shut down in the past and you were not open or receptive to hearing His voice. That is why the Holy Spirit says, in Hebrews 3:7-8 NLT: "Today when you hear his voice, don't harden your hearts as Israel did when they rebelled, when they tested me in the wilderness."

Prophetic word for your heart:

You have been on My mind. My thoughts are for your good; the blessings of life that are yours. Do not be dismayed or afraid because all will work together for your good. All things that seem to work against you will bless you in the end and raise you to new heights and new places.

Meditation-Prayer-Reflection
DAY THIRTY

How did God speak to you today?

_____
_____
_____
_____
_____
_____
_____
_____

What are your thoughts now?

___

___

___

___

___

___

___

How will you pray?

___

___

___

___

Day Thirty-One

The Power Of An Excellent Spirit

The thief does not come except to steal, and to kill, and to destroy. I have come that they may have life, and that they may have it more abundantly.

John 10:10

Luke 8:41-56 AMPC: "And there came a man named Jairus, who had for a long time been a director of the synagogue; and falling at the feet of Jesus, he begged Him to come to his house, for he had an only daughter, about twelve years of age, and she was dying. As Jesus went, the people pressed together around Him almost suffocating Him. And a woman who had suffered from a flow of blood for twelve years and had spent all her living upon physicians, and could not be healed by anyone, came up behind Him and touched the fringe of His garment, and immediately her flow of blood ceased. And Jesus said, "Who is it who touched Me?" When all were denying it, Peter and those who were with him said, Master, the multitudes surround You and press You on every side! But Jesus said, someone did touch Me; for I perceived that healing power has gone forth from Me. And when the woman saw that she had not escaped notice, she came up trembling, and, falling down before Him, she declared in the presence of all the people for what reason she had touched Him and how she had been instantly cured. And He said to her, Daughter, your faith your confidence and trust in Me has made you well! Go enter into peace untroubled, undisturbed well-being."

There is hope for you even though your struggle has been long and hard. Sometimes the difficulties and sicknesses that come to wear you down in life seem to be without end. You must know and believe that though your struggle is real and the season long, you are not forgotten. Will you be made whole? Come and see the Master is waiting for you.

Prophet word for your heart today:

I have not turned a deaf ear towards you. I have come to you, to reach out My hand to pull you up from your weakness. Remember I am the God of the living and I bring good tidings to you. I will feed you as a mother feeds her young child. I will meet you at the top because you cannot stay in a holding place. I have reserved your status; your position is safe with Me. I have fought for you. Your enemies are defeated. The fight is over; stand up and see My glory and feel My great power. I Am that I Am!

Meditation-Prayer-Reflection

DAY THIRTY-ONE

How did God speak to you today?

_____
_____
_____
_____
_____
_____
_____

What are your thoughts now?

_____
_____
_____
_____
_____
_____
_____

How will you pray?

_____
_____
_____
_____

Conclusion

Congratulations, you made it through this 31-day journey into the process and development of your new prophetic encounter. It is my prayer that this 31day devotional book has been an inspiration, motivation, and revelation to you. Prophetic Heartbeats was written through prophetic revelation from the Lord, to touch masses of people with the prophetic word. I pray that these Prophetic Heartbeats have enlightened you as a reader, stirring you into new possibilities and ideas that you had not considered. The opportunities and dreams within you are endless and waiting to take you into exciting and unlimited places of your prophetic life. Your life is amazing because you are in relationship and fellowship with the amazing God Almighty. Your God is able to do exceeding, abundantly, above all that you could ask, think, hope, dream or imagine.

I hope that your heart was refreshed, renewed, and invigorated with a new inspiration of divine perspectives to take you higher and in new directions. Remember these prophetic words are not just for thirty days. Prophetic Heartbeats will trigger a new wave of thoughts and decisions that will catapult your prayer life into new spiritual portals and intercessory breakthroughs. As this happens, they will free you from the status-quo of life.

The spiritual doors are open, and your heart is refreshed; the time to move forward is now. It is your time to step out of the status quo and launch out into the deep. Let the Spirit of the Lord enrapture you and reveal great things of which you do not know. Please go back over some of the prophetic teachings and prophetic heartbeats. Then allow the Holy Spirit to navigate you into a whole new life that has been waiting for you.

You are now ready to move into a new norm, so don't go back into the old norm for your life. The Holy Spirit has been speaking to you throughout these 31 days, so stay open, ready, and focused on where you are going and not where you have been. There is a new you that is now awakened with fresh insight and foresight to give you real oversight of your life from God's perspective.

Finally, what you have learned, felt, and thought, you should have written down, so you can go back and reflect upon it. Make it your new focus in prophetic prayer. Also make it your new confession and spiritual goal to reach out into the outer limits. Your dreams are not dead; they have only been lying dormant under the rubbish of 'life stuff' that tries to hide your prophetic future and divine destiny.

Your Finale Thoughts

_____
_____
_____
_____
_____
_____
_____
_____
_____
_____
_____
_____

www.ingramcontent.com/pod-product-compliance
Lightning Source LLC
LaVergne TN
LVHW051949060526
838201LV00059B/3577